DATE			

AMAZING ARCHAEOLOGISTS

True Stories of Astounding Archaeological Discoveries

Fiona Macdonald

Chicago, Illinois

To contact Capstone Global Library please
phone 800-747-4992, or visit our website
www.capstonepub.com

Produced for Raintree by
White-Thomson Publishing Ltd
www.wtpub.co.uk
+44 (0)843 208 7460

Edited by Sonya Newland
Designed by Tim Mayer
Concept design by Ian Winton
Illustrations by Stefan Chabluk
Originated by Capstone Global Library Ltd
Printed and bound in China by CTPS

Library of Congress Cataloging-in-Publication Data
Macdonald, Fiona.
  Amazing archaeologists: true stories of
astounding archaeological discoveries/ Fiona
Macdonald.
      pages cm.—(Ultimate adventurers)
  Includes bibliographical references and index.
  ISBN 978-1-4109-5419-0 (hb)—ISBN 978-1-4109-
6299-7 (pb) 1. Archaeologists—Juvenile literature.
2. Excavations (Archaeology)—Juvenile literature.
I. Title.

  CC107.M34 2014
  930.1—dc23 2013016812

17 16 15 14 13
10 9 8 7 6 5 4 3 2 1

Acknowledgments
The author and publisher are grateful to
the following for permission to reproduce
copyright material:
Alamy p. 41 (Mo Fini); Corbis pp. 7 (Bettmann),
9 (Chris Melzer/dpa), 10 (National Geographic
Society), 11 (Ralph White), 13 (Didier Dutheil/
Sygma), 15 (Reuters), 16 (Bettmann), 27 (Reuters),
38 (Vienna Report Agency/Sygma); Dreamstime:
pp. 26–27 (Danbreckwoldt), 28 (Prehor), 33
(Jplanken); Getty Images pp. 5, 12 (AFP), 19
(Time & Life Pictures), 20 (UIG), 23 (National
Geographic), 29 (Gamma-Rapho), 36, 40 (Maria
Stenzel); Press Association p. 17 (Mike Hettwer/
AP); Shutterstock pp. 4 (Dmitriy Yakovlev), 6
(Amy Nichole Harris), 31 (Hung Chung Chih), 32–
33 (Ajancso), 34 (Hung Chung Chih), 8–39 (Richie
Ji); Superstock p. 22 (Tips Images); Wikipedia
pp. 21 (Eric Bronder), 25t (Hans Hillewaert/
CC-BY-SA-3.0), 25b (The Official White House
Photostream), 35 (Wit).

Cover photograph of gold mask from Sipán
reproduced with permission of National
Geographic/Getty Images.

Every effort has been made to contact copyright
holders of any material reproduced in this book.
Any omissions will be rectified in subsequent
printings if notice is given to the publisher.

All the Internet addresses (URLs) given in this
book were valid at the time of going to press.
However, due to the dynamic nature of the
Internet, some addresses may have changed,
or sites may have changed or ceased to exist
since publication. While the author and publisher
regret any inconvenience this may cause readers,
no responsibility for any such changes can be
accepted by either the author or the publisher.

CONTENTS

A Passion for the Past 4

Robert Ballard—Ocean Explorer 8

Paul Sereno—Fossil Finder 12

Walter Alva—Tomb Defender 18

Zahi Hawass—Secrets from the Sand 24

The Terracotta Warriors—
an Underground Army 30

Constanza Ceruti—
Mountaineer Archaeologist 36

Timeline 42

Quiz 43

Glossary 44

Find Out More 46

Index 48

A PASSION FOR THE PAST

Have you ever dreamed of traveling back in time, to meet famous heroes, brave warriors, wise queens, or your own long-dead ancestors? Have you wandered round museums admiring giant statues, glittering jewels, and mysterious mummies? Do you wonder who made them—and how, when, where, and why?

Digging for History

If the answer to any of these questions is "yes," then you share a vision with many adventurous archaeologists—men and women with a passion to find out about the past. These people travel the globe in search of lost cities and buried treasures. They decipher ancient carvings and dusty documents. And they dig up smelly old sewers and burial grounds.

From tiny ancient bones to whole cities, archaeological discoveries help us piece together the past.

Howard Carter

In 1922, the British archaeologist Howard Carter discovered one of the world's most famous ancient treasures: the tomb of the boy-king Tutankhamun, who ruled Egypt over 3,000 years ago. Carter was dazzled when he first peered inside the tomb—it was full of "wonderful things."

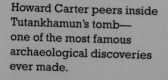

Howard Carter peers inside Tutankhamun's tomb— one of the most famous archaeological discoveries ever made.

A World of Discovery

At the same time, archaeologists learn exciting new skills and experiment with the latest technology to find out what life was like long ago. Their work takes them on adventures to all kinds of places— from deep, dark oceans to high mountaintops.

Then and Now

Today, archaeologists use modern technology in their work. Nearly 100 years ago, however, Carter and his team discovered Tutankhamun's treasures by simple excavation. They cleared away about 10 feet (3 meters) of sandy, rocky soil—and some old huts— before uncovering the steps that led to Tut's tomb.

Lost—and Forgotten?

What happened to the remains of people who lived long ago? They got buried under roads and buildings, crushed by earthquakes, or swept away by floods. Some were plowed up and scattered by farmers, or covered by jungle trees and vines.

Ancient treasures were left in tombs alongside the bodies of important people such as kings, or thrown into pools and bogs as offerings to the gods. A few precious objects were hidden away for safekeeping by owners who never came back for them. Some were stolen. Some simply got lost.

The secret Inca city of Machu Picchu in Peru was explored by adventurer Hiram Bingham in 1911.

Treasure-hunters

Although all this evidence from past times disappeared from view, it was not forgotten. For hundreds of years, explorers and treasure-hunters tried to find it. Some, like the American Roy Chapman Andrews (1884–1960) spent their lives searching in wild, lonely places. Andrews roamed the deserts of Mongolia, hunting for fossil dinosaurs—he was the first scientist to find a nest of fossilized dinosaur eggs.

In 1923, Roy Chapman Andrews found a nest containing the eggs of a dinosaur called *Oviraptor*, whose name means "egg thief."

Percy Fawcett

British adventurer Percy Fawcett (1867–1925) had some very odd ideas. He thought that a beautiful ghost was calling him to make discoveries in the rain forest. So he went to Brazil, hoping to find a lost "city of gold" and to start a new religion. He disappeared. To this day, nobody knows what happened to him.

ROBERT BALLARD
OCEAN EXPLORER

American Robert Ballard chose one of the world's most challenging environments for his adventures: deep under the sea. In a long and successful career, he has taken part in over 120 pioneering investigations.

Ballard has made some amazing discoveries: weird underwater creatures, deep-sea vents and volcanoes, and the remains of many famous shipwrecks, including the *Titanic*. Today, he still investigates the underwater world.

Inspired by Nemo

Born in 1942 in Wichita, Kansas, Ballard grew up in San Diego on the Californian coast. He was fascinated by the nearby ocean. His childhood hero was Captain Nemo—a fictional underwater explorer in Jules Verne's novel *Twenty Thousand Leagues Under the Sea*. As a teenager, Ballard spent a summer on a sea-exploration ship. After this, he knew he wanted a career studying the oceans.

The *Titanic* sank where the sea is 13,100 feet (4,000 meters) deep. Until explorers like Ballard found ways of searching the deepest parts of the oceans, no one could find the remains of the great ship.

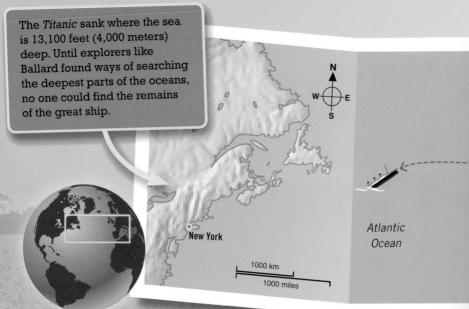

New York

Atlantic Ocean

1000 km

1000 miles

Robert Ballard makes a speech describing his discovery of the *Titanic*. The picture shows the upper deck of the great liner.

Ballard went to college, then served in the US Navy, working closely with experts at the world-famous Woods Hole Oceanographic Institution in Massachusetts. While there, he helped develop new submersibles—machines that would help explore the depths of the oceans.

Belfast
Queenstown
Southampton
Cherbourg

TOOLS of the TRADE

Submersibles are like miniature submarines, carrying two or three people. They are fitted with bright lights, cameras, and robot arms to grab samples. Sometimes, they are linked to surface ships by long cables carrying electrical power and communications signals.

Deep and Dangerous

Ballard made his first submersible dive in 1969, and then took part in many expeditions to explore the ocean floor. These dives were slow —submersibles rose or descended at around 1 mile (1.6 kilometers) per hour. They were also extremely dangerous. In deep water, the pressure could be 250 times greater than on dry land. There was a real risk that the submersibles and their crews would be crushed. Ballard worked with engineers to develop ROVs (remotely operated vehicles) that could be controlled by operators safely on board ship or on shore.

The Sinking of the *Titanic*

In 1912, the huge ocean liner RMS *Titanic* sank after hitting an iceberg on its maiden (first) voyage from Southampton in England to New York. More than 1,500 passengers and crew on the ship were drowned. This was the world's worst disaster at sea.

A year after finding the *Titanic* wreckage in 1985, Ballard made a deep and daring dive in *Alvin*, a specially strengthened submersible (shown here over the bow of the ship).

In complete darkness, two miles below the surface, searchlights lit up the *Titanic*'s towering hull. The sight was tragic, wonderful—and scary!

Finding the *Titanic*

In 1985, Ballard started searching for the wreck of the most famous ship of all time—the *Titanic*. He used the ROV *Argo* to scan a wide area of seabed, and amazingly he found the wreck! The next year, he sent ROV *Jason Junior* to explore deep inside the *Titanic*'s huge hull. The images it sent back of the wreck became world-famous, and inspired a blockbuster movie.

Young Explorers

Ballard went on exploring, finding World War II battleships, ancient Roman cargo boats, and much more. In 1989, after thousands of children wrote to him asking to join in his adventures, he set up the Jason Project. This was intended to encourage young people to study science and technology.

TOOLS OF THE TRADE

ROVs like *Argo* use digital cameras and acoustic scanners to create images of underwater objects. They send continuous information to computers on ship or shore. They can operate in very deep water, and explore places that are too small or dangerous for submersibles.

PAUL SERENO

FOSSIL FINDER

Millions of years ago, long before humans lived on Earth, dinosaurs roamed the planet. These amazing beasts have fascinated scientists and explorers since their bones were first discovered nearly 200 years ago. Dinosaurs are one of American scientist Paul Sereno's favorite research topics.

Sereno is a university professor and a world-famous explorer. He also helps run Project Exploration, a program to inspire and help schoolchildren to study science.

Scientist-detectives

Scientists like Paul Sereno are called paleontologists (people who study prehistoric life). They need a wide range of knowledge—including biology, anatomy (bodies), geology (rocks), chemistry, engineering, and mathematics. They also need inquiring minds and good detective skills!

Mary Anning

One of the earliest fossil experts was Mary Anning, from Dorset, England. Born in 1799, she studied fossils and shells that she found on the seaside cliffs near her home, and sold them to collectors. Her life story inspired the tongue-twister "She sells sea-shells on the sea-shore."

Natural History

Born in Illinois in 1957, Sereno did not get a good education. "School failed me," he said. He became an artist, learning how to make careful, accurate observations to bring his paintings and drawings to life. He moved to New York City, where, one day, he visited the famous American Museum of Natural History.

The museum is a treasure-house of information about the natural world, with displays about ocean life, birds and reptiles, and meteorites from space. It also has a magnificent collection of dinosaur fossils. Sereno was captivated by what he saw, especially the ancient bones and fossils. He longed to find out more.

Sereno has made expeditions to many different lands and made some remarkable discoveries. Here, he and his team are uncovering two fossilized dinosaurs—*Afrovenator* and *Jobaria*.

Early Discoveries

The best fossils are often found in deserts, canyons, cliffs, and mountain ranges, where they have not been disturbed by humans or animals. Sereno's hunt for dinosaurs led him to many of these wild and lonely places. He made his first exciting discovery in 1988, in the dry, dusty badlands of Argentina. There, he uncovered the fossil bones of dinosaurs that lived around 225 million years ago, some of the earliest known species.

Desert Adventures

In 1997, Sereno began to explore another desert—the vast, windswept Sahara in Niger, West Africa. Temperatures there reached 125 degrees Fahrenheit (52 degrees Celsius) during the day. At night, it was bitterly cold. There were hardly any roads, very little water, and no bathrooms. The desert was also filled with dangerous insects! The explorers had to carry all their food, fuel, tents, tools, and medical supplies.

This map shows where Sereno and his team discovered the fossilized bones of Supercroc, in West Africa.

A Prehistoric Giant

Supercroc measured 40 feet (12 meters) long, weighed about 9 tons, and had eyeballs as big as melons. Its huge jaws boasted over 100 teeth!

The skull of Supercroc, *Sarcosuchus imperator* (meaning "flesh-crocodile emperor") next to the skull of a modern croc. Supercroc was not related to today's crocodiles, although it looked like one.

Supercroc!

Despite these difficulties, Sereno and his team were determined to uncover the prehistoric secrets of the Sahara. They found fossilized dinosaurs of many different shapes and sizes. But in 2000 they really struck gold. Deep below the desert sand, they discovered a monster that no one had seen before—a crocodile-shaped fossil that was 110 million years old. They nicknamed it Supercroc!

TOOLS OF THE TRADE

Once a dinosaur fossil has been found, it is usually taken to a laboratory. There, scientists clean it very carefully, using delicate, sharp-pointed, vibrating tools, to remove a few grains of rock at a time. After this, the bones are fitted together to try to make a complete skeleton.

Human Remains

Between 2003 and 2011, Sereno led a team of paleontologists on several trips across the Sahara to Gobero in Niger. As usual, they were hunting for ancient bones, but this time the bones did not belong to prehistoric beasts—they were human. On an earlier trip, Sereno's team had found signs of human remains. Now they wanted to find out more about these ancient people.

Mary Leakey holds up casts of the footprints she found in Africa.

Mary Leakey

In 1978, Mary Leakey, a researcher from Britain, made an amazing discovery. She found fossilized footprints at Laetoli, in Tanzania, Africa. They were 3.6 million years old! They revealed that hominids (early human ancestors) had walked upright instead of running on all fours, as scientists had previously thought.

Tests showed that the bones were between 10,000 and 5,000 years old. Here, a woman and two children are curled up together.

Secrets of the Sands

Very gently, the team brushed away the sand. To their astonishment, they uncovered more than 200 human skeletons. Stone arrowheads, clay cooking pots, fishhooks, blue beads, and hippo-tusk jewelry were all found close by. There were also bones from creatures that had been hunted and eaten: fish, turtles, elephants, snakes, and frogs.

Sereno had found the earliest-known burial ground in Africa! His discovery also showed that the Sahara had not always been a desert. Once, there had been lakes filled by rainfall, and grass and trees. The lake water had supported wildlife and human families. But all had died out or moved away long ago because the climate changed.

WALTER ALVA

TOMB DEFENDER

Would you risk your life to save ancient relics? That's what Walter Alva did! He braved angry tomb-robbers armed with guns—and discovered the treasures of the Lord of Sipán.

The Moche People

Born in 1951, in Contumaza, Peru, Alva trained as an archaeologist. In 1987, he was working near the village of Sipán. This was a remote place—poor and underdeveloped. Many local people could not find work; their families were hungry.

Peru

A N D E S   M O U N T A I N S

Sipán

Pacific
Ocean

N
W · E
S

100 km
100 miles

■ Moche civilization
● Archaeological sites

A map showing where the Moche people lived in South America, and the location of the tomb of the Lord of Sipán.

Then and Now

Tomb-robbing is not a new crime. Over 4,000 years ago, thieves hunting treasures buried beside dead bodies broke into pyramid tombs in ancient Egypt. Often these tombs had spells and curses written at their entrances, warning people to stay away. But the ancient Egyptian tomb-raiders paid no attention to these curses from the dead.

Alva knew that, long ago, Sipán had been home to the ancient and mysterious Moche people. They were hunters, farmers, and craftsmen. They made pottery and built huge pyramid temples. But no one knew anything more about them.

Loot from Long Ago

The Moche were powerful from around 100 BCE until around CE 700. After this time, they were weakened by famines and attacked by invaders. Eventually the civilization collapsed.

However, the goods the Moche people made survived in and around their half-ruined temples. Over the years, local people began raiding the Moche tombs, stealing the treasures to sell them to collectors. These tomb-robbers did not care what damage they caused to the ancient sites they looted.

Walter Alva (right) and a fellow archaeologist examine a find in the ancient tomb of a Moche warrior-priest.

19

The Broken Pyramid Temple

One night in 1987, a group of tomb-robbers finally finished digging. Coughing and stumbling, they crept through the darkness. At last they were inside the great Huaca Rajada (Broken Pyramid Temple) at Sipán. Cautiously, they lowered themselves into a deep, shadowy chamber—and found that it was empty! They decided to leave, but they knew it would be difficult to climb back out the way they had come in. Perhaps there was a doorway?

It's Raining Gold!

The robbers tapped the chamber walls with sticks. They could not find any sign of a doorway. Then one of them poked his stick at the ceiling. Suddenly, gold and silver came raining down from a secret store above him.

This picture shows what the temple pyramid at Sipán may have looked like when the Moche people lived there.

The robbers had not yet reached the tomb of the Lord of Sipán. All the precious objects buried with him—as well as his mummified body—were found intact.

For three nights, the robbers kept returning to the chamber, carrying off the treasure. But then they quarreled over who should have the best of it. One angry robber betrayed the rest to the police. Amazed by what they found, the police called in an expert—Walter Alva. When Alva saw the treasures, he was amazed. The gold and silver jewelry was so beautiful, he had never seen anything like it before.

Burial Companions

The treasures found by the robbers belonged to a powerful ruler, the Lord of Sipán. Soon, Alva found the lord's tomb—undamaged! The lord had been buried with three wives, a child, a lookout, two warriors, a dog, two llamas, and more than 400 precious holy objects.

Saving the Treasures of Sipán

Alva knew that he must act quickly to find out what else was hidden inside the pyramid temple and stop any more robberies. With hardly any money, he planned a swift—but careful—excavation. He must save the treasures of Sipán!

Archaeologists had to work hard and fast to excavate the Moche site at the Huaca Rajada.

Splendid objects, such as this gold figure of a warrior lord, were discovered in the tomb at Sipán.

However, the local people were suspicious. They accused Alva of taking "their" gold. Angry mobs surrounded the site of his archaeological dig. They threatened Alva and the other workers on the site. Police fired tear gas to drive away the robbers. In another incident, a tomb-robber was shot dead.

Pride in the Past

What could Alva do? The police could not protect him forever. So he invited the protesters to come and see what he had discovered. He told them he did not want to take their treasures; instead, he was trying to preserve their heritage. The leader of the mob agreed to trust him.

Alva and the protesters also found a way of using the treasures to bring money to the region. Today, Sipán is one of Peru's top visitor attractions. Some local people are still very poor, but others have jobs in the tourist industry or work in the two new museums that display the amazing treasures of Sipán.

ZAHI HAWASS

SECRETS FROM THE SAND

For years, Zahi Hawass was one of the world's most influential archaeologists. A forceful, controversial character, he spent his career uncovering Egypt's past. He discovered a royal statue and a lost pyramid, and helped save the mysterious Great Sphinx. "I *am* Egyptian antiquities," he said.

This map shows some of the most famous ancient sites in Egypt, including the pyramids and the Valley of the Kings.

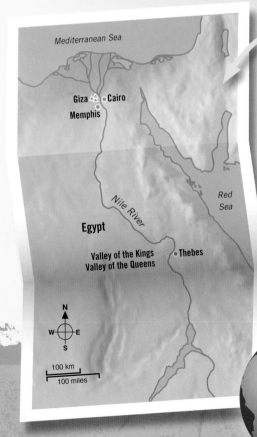

Mediterranean Sea

Giza • Cairo
Memphis

Red Sea

Nile River

Egypt

Valley of the Kings • Thebes
Valley of the Queens

N
W E
S

100 km
100 miles

Hawass's Rise...

Born in Damietta, Egypt, in 1947, Hawass planned to become an attorney. But after learning about his country's fascinating history, he changed his mind and studied archaeology instead. In the 1980s, he began to work for the Egyptian government. His fame grew and he became a well-known media personality, writing bestselling books and appearing on television.

> "He cleaned up the sites, built tourist facilities and museums, organized exhibitions abroad, and brought Egyptian antiquities into the center of worldwide attention."
> **Dieter Arnold, Metropolitan Museum, New York**

...and Fall

In 2003, Hawass hit the headlines by demanding that museums in other countries return ancient Egyptian objects, such as the famous Rosetta Stone, to his country. He added that he would "make life miserable" if they refused. In 2011, after bitter quarrels with Egypt's new prime minister, Hawass stopped working for the government. But he still cares passionately about—and works to preserve—Egypt's past.

The Rosetta Stone

The Rosetta Stone is an ancient stone slab discovered in Egypt in 1799. The stone has three types of writing on it: Greek, Demotic, and hieroglyphs. Before its discovery, no one could read hieroglyphs, but afterward people could compare the hieroglyphs to the other two languages and work out what they meant.

Zahi Hawass (left) takes President Barack Obama on a tour of the pyramids in Egypt.

25

Robot Exploration

The Great Pyramid at Giza was built around 2560 BCE as a tomb for the Egyptian pharaoh (king) Khufu. In 1992, Hawass organized the first robot exploration deep inside this ancient building. The robot crawled 200 feet (60 meters) along a narrow shaft (tunnel), but then its way was blocked by a carved door and it could go no farther.

In 2002, as millions of fascinated viewers around the world watched on television, a second robot found another doorway. After this, though, it was nearly a decade before a third robot was sent into the pyramid in 2011. This one found hieroglyphs. Some scholars thought that the tomb-builders may have made the narrow tunnels so that the pharaoh's spirit could fly freely. But Hawass thought they might be a pathway to a secret chamber.

Massive, magnificent, mysterious—the Great Pyramid at Giza in Egypt is one of the Seven Wonders of the Ancient World.

The Tomb-builders' Cemetery

Hawass worked on another pyramid project with his American colleague Mark Lerner. Hawass believed that the graves of the people who built the pyramids at Giza would be somewhere nearby. Excavations provided exciting new evidence about these workers. In a huge, hidden cemetery, the archaeologists found statues, carvings, and texts commemorating the dead builders. They also found many objects that the workers had used in their everyday lives.

A robot is sent into one of the small tunnels that run through the Great Pyramid, trying to explore the mysteries of this ancient monument.

The Pyramid-builders

In the past, many people thought that the pyramids were built by slaves or Hebrew captives. A few people claimed that they were made by aliens from outer space! But Hawass and Lerner proved that the pyramids were constructed by skilled Egyptians, helped by farmers who were let off paying taxes in return for their work.

Tutankhamun's Tomb

In 1922, the untouched tomb of the pharaoh Tutankhamun was discovered in the Valley of the Kings in Egypt. The treasures that archaeologists found there were amazing, but still no one knew what King Tutankhamun was like as a ruler, and no one was certain who his family was. There were no surviving stone carvings or texts written on papyrus to tell his life story.

Years later, in 2005, Hawass set out to find out more about this mysterious pharaoh. He wanted to satisfy his own curiosity, as well as that of millions of people around the world who were fascinated by Tutankhamun.

The stunning gold funeral mask is one of the most famous treasures discovered in the tomb of the pharaoh Tutankhamun.

"People often ask me, 'well, it's not really as exciting as Indiana Jones, now is it?' I reply, 'to an archaeologist, yes, it certainly is!'"
Zahi Hawass

Family Reunion

Hawass and his team examined Tutankhamun's mummy using CT-scan technology. They discovered that the pharaoh was only a teenager when he died, and that he had a badly broken left leg. Although he was skinny, he had eaten well during his lifetime. This was more than anyone knew before.

Five years later, other experts studied some DNA taken from Tutankahmun's body. They compared their findings with samples from other Egyptian mummies—and found Tutankamun's father! They also identified his grandparents, his mother, and his wife. "This will open to us a new era," Hawass said. "I am very proud of what we have done."

Among many other treasures, Hawass found hundreds of beautiful golden mummies buried in the desert— Egypt's most spectacular discovery since Tutankhamun's tomb.

THE TERRACOTTA WARRIORS
AN UNDERGROUND ARMY

Lintong county, near Xi'an in China, has a dry, dusty climate. In 1974, a group of farmers in the region needed a new source of water, so they began to dig a well. While digging, they hit something round and hollow. At first they thought it was a pottery jug, but it turned out to be the head of a life-size model warrior!

Digging Deeper

As the farmers dug deeper, they discovered bronze arrowheads and thousands more pieces of baked clay called terracotta. A worker at a nearby museum heard about these finds and hurried to see them. At the same time, a local reporter passed the news to Chinese government officials. They sent a team of experts to the area to investigate.

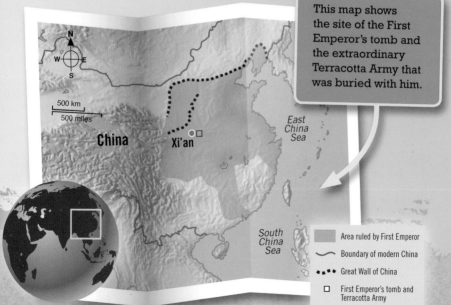

This map shows the site of the First Emperor's tomb and the extraordinary Terracotta Army that was buried with him.

500 km
500 miles

China

Xi'an

East China Sea

South China Sea

Area ruled by First Emperor

Boundary of modern China

Great Wall of China

First Emperor's tomb and Terracotta Army

The Great Wall of China was built to defend Qin Shi Huang's empire. He also ordered miles of roads and canals to be built.

On Guard Forever

When they arrived at the site, the experts were amazed. Hundreds of terracotta warriors were being uncovered. Each one was unique, with his own facial features, hairstyle, clothes, and weapons. Every figure was a masterpiece, and no one had seen anything like them before.

Today, experts think that a whole army—about 8,000 statues—was buried near Xi'an to guard the tomb of the emperor Qin Shi Huang. These watchful warriors stood there undisturbed for more than 2,000 years before the farmers found them by accident.

The First Emperor

Qin Shi Huang (died 210 BCE) was the first emperor of China. He was greatly respected—and greatly feared! Qin joined all the warring Chinese states into a single strong nation. He passed strict new laws and introduced new coins and new ways of writing. He burned books he disagreed with, and killed the people who wrote them!

Rescue Mission

The warriors were wonderful, but archaeologists realized that they would need a great deal of care and conservation. Although everyone wanted to uncover as many statues as possible and restore them to their former glory, this would be a huge job.

The faces and bodies of many warriors had been smashed long ago, when rebel armies tried—but failed—to raid the emperor's tomb. Putting the pieces together would not be easy. The bright paint decorating the warriors' clothes peeled off as soon as each one was uncovered. Soot from nearby factories threatened to wear away the terracotta, and moisture from eager visitors' breath quickly turned the clay moldy.

Missing History

The ancient Chinese historian Sima Qian (145–86 BCE) wrote that 700,000 people worked for many years to build the emperor's tomb and burial mound. Strangely, though, he does not mention the terracotta warriors...

Archaeologists slowly excavated vast pits around the thousands of terracotta statues.

Longer Than a Lifetime

The conservation task was so huge that it needed teams of dedicated people, each with their own special skills. Even so, archaeologists said that it might take longer than a lifetime—maybe 100 years—to uncover and preserve all the thousands of warriors, and investigate the historic area around them.

Archaeologists were also keen to investigate the huge, grim mound of earth above the emperor's tomb, which stood close by. It was over 2,000 years old, but had never been excavated. What secrets might it reveal?

As well as the warriors themselves, archaeologists uncovered horses and chariots also made of terracotta.

Chinese archaeologists have now started working again to uncover, restore, and preserve the amazing terracotta warriors.

Saying No

When danger threatens, the boldest, bravest, and best explorers always stop and think. In 1986, because many terracotta warriors were in such a fragile condition, leaders of the Chinese team announced that they would stop digging for a while. They thought it would be safer if the warriors remained untouched, underground. Excavations did not start again until 2009. By this time, scientists had found better ways of preserving the paint and protecting the terracotta.

More Models

Archaeologists have uncovered life-size model dancers, acrobats, and musicians close to the terracotta warriors, together with beautiful metal birds from a model zoo. All were designed to delight the dead emperor in his tomb.

Rest in Peace

Chinese archaeologists have also decided not to investigate the emperor's tall tomb-mound, although they believe that it may be full of fabulous treasures. This is partly because they respect Qin Shi Huang as the founder of their nation. But they also do not want to damage the tomb or the wonderful things buried there. They hope that, in the future, new technology will let them see what is hidden without digging. That way, the mighty Qin Shi Huang—commander of the Terracotta Army—can continue to rest in peace.

Like a manmade miniature mountain, the mound containing the emperor's tomb towers 377 feet (115 meters) high.

"I have a dream that one day science can develop so that we can tell what is here without disturbing the emperor...we cannot unearth his tomb just because archaeologists or people doing tourism want to know what is buried there."
Wu Yongqi, Director of the Museum of the Terracotta Army

CONSTANZA CERUTI

MOUNTAINEER ARCHAEOLOGIST

Most archaeologists look downward to find treasures from the past—they search below ground or under the sea. Not Constanza Ceruti! She looks upward, to high mountaintops where ancient peoples worshiped their gods. Ceruti is one the world's few female mountaineer archaeologists, and has climbed more than 100 peaks over 16,400 feet (5,000 meters) high.

Early Inspiration

Born in Buenos Aires, Argentina, in 1973, Ceruti climbed her first high hill when she was just 14 years old. From the top, she saw wonderful views of distant mountain ranges rising up toward the sky. She longed to explore them, and says that the memory of that early climb still inspires her today.

Constanza Ceruti (on the far left in this picture) is honored at a ceremony celebrating "Women of Discovery."

Aiming High

In college, Ceruti studied anthropology (the science of cultures and lifestyles) and archaeology. She was especially interested in the ancient Inca people, who ruled over a mighty empire in the Andes mountains of South America from around 1300 to 1532. In 1999, Ceruti and the American explorer Johan Reinhard set off on an expedition. Their goal? To reach the top of Mount Llullaillaco at the border between Argentina and Chile—the highest archaeological site in the world.

"These mountains are so remote. Not only am I often the first archaeologist on the site but the first modern person to arrive since the Incas."
Constanza Ceruti

Peru

Bolivia

SOUTH

AMERICA

Mount Llullaillaco

Pacific Ocean

Chile

ANDES MOUNTAINS

Argentina

250 km
250 miles

Preparing for the Climb

Although Reinhard and Ceruti were experienced mountaineers, their expedition was still risky. High peaks like Llullaillaco are a very hostile environment—a frozen world of bitter cold, blinding snowstorms, and winds that howl at over 70 miles (113 kilometers) per hour. Before starting their climb, expedition members had to spend a month in the mountains, so that their bodies could adapt to the harsh conditions.

Ötzi is an example of an ice mummy, where a body is preserved naturally because of extreme cold.

Iceman Ötzi

In 1991, hikers exploring the mountains between Austria and Italy discovered a man's body, frozen in ice about 10,500 feet (3,210 meters) above sea level. Scientists named him Ötzi. He may have been a chieftain who was killed by an arrow around 3300 BCE.

Eventually, after a long climb, Ceruti and the team reached the summit of Llullaillaco. It was a fearful place: bleak, barren, and icy. The explorers knew that the ancient Inca people left gifts for their gods, sometimes human sacrifices, high on the mountaintops. The team camped there for a week, eagerly searching for remains of the past. But they found nothing.

A Vital Clue

They were getting ready to give up and make the long climb back down the mountain, when someone suddenly spotted a tiny carved animal. It was evidence that the Incas had been there—and that they had left behind treasures! Close by, half hidden under fallen rocks, the team discovered the bodies of two girls and a boy. Five hundred years old, and perfectly preserved by the freezing temperatures, these children were Inca sacrifices.

High in the mountains there is little oxygen in the air, which makes it hard to breathe.

"When we found the mummies, I remember a profound silence falling over the group. It is so humbling to look into the eyes of another human being from half a millennium [500 years] ago."
Constanza Ceruti

A Precious Gift to the Gods

The children found on the mountaintop had been sacrificed because the Incas valued them. They were beautiful and strong. Their lives were precious. They came from high-ranking families, and if they had lived they would have been powerful people. One of them, the eldest girl, was being trained as a royal wife. All this made them special treasures to give to the gods. They had been well-fed and cared for before they were left to die.

> "We have a lot to learn from mountain people regarding having a deeper connection with the natural world and the care that is needed."
> **Constanza Ceruti**

What the Children Tell Us

Today, archaeologists treasure the bodies of the children found on Llullaillaco for other reasons. They are the best-preserved Inca mummies ever found. The Incas left no written records, so the children's frozen bodies provide valuable information about their ethnic origins, customs, food and nutrition, living conditions, clothing, hairstyles, state of health, and typical diseases. The holy offerings left beside the children also help us understand the customs and beliefs of the Inca people.

Aged between about six and 15, the Inca children were dressed in fine clothes and surrounded by holy offerings.

El Niño

Some archaeologists think that the children were sacrificed to ask the gods to send better weather. In the past, just like today, the west coast of South America suffered from extreme floods and droughts caused by El Niño. This is a period of time when currents of water in the Pacific Ocean become unusually warm. It is linked to changes in air pressure, which often cause very bad weather.

Today, some people living in the Andes still make offerings to the mountain gods.

TIMELINE

1911	Hiram Bingham explores the Incan city of Machu Picchu
1912	RMS *Titanic* hits an iceberg and sinks
1922	Howard Carter discovers Tutankhamun's tomb in Egypt
1923	Roy Chapman Andrews finds fossilized dinosaur eggs
1925	Percy Fawcett disappears in the South American rain forest
1974	Farmers near Xi'an, China, discover the Terracotta Army
1978	Mary Leakey discovers fossilized hominid footprints in Tanzania, Africa
1985	Robert Ballard discovers the wreck of the *Titanic*
1986	Chinese experts halt the excavation of the terracotta warriors until better ways can be found of conserving the statues
1987	Walter Alva uncovers the tomb of the Lord of Sipán
1988	Paul Sereno finds fossils of the oldest-known dinosaurs
1990	Zahi Hawass discovers the cemetery of the pyramid-builders at Giza, Egypt
1992	Zahi Hawass leads the first robot exploration inside the Great Pyramid, Egypt
1997	Paul Sereno finds the first fossils of "Supercroc" in the Sahara Desert, Africa
1999	Constanza Ceruti and Johan Reinhard discover three ice-mummy Incan children at the summit of Mount Llullaillaco
2003	Paul Sereno sets off to discover a "lost" community in the Sahara Desert, Niger, Africa
2010	Laser survey reveals Mayan city hidden in the rain forest at Caracol, Belize

QUIZ

DO YOU HAVE WHAT IT TAKES TO BE AN ARCHAEOLOGICAL ADVENTURER?

Are you passionate about the past?

a I've studied history and I'd love to travel back in time.

b I like history, but I'm just as interested in what's happening today.

c I don't often think about people who are dead and gone.

Do you long to go exploring?

a I want to learn explorer skills and go to faraway places to hunt for historical remains.

b I'm interested in exploring the history of my family and homeland.

c I love visiting other countries on vacation.

Have you got the skills for excavating?

a I'm neat, careful, and hardworking. I've studied in museums, so I can recognize ancient objects.

b Digging sounds fun, but I don't know how to draw maps or record finds.

c I'm afraid I'm rather clumsy. I drop things and break them!

Are you a born detective?

a I'm observant and quick-thinking. I'd like hunting for evidence.

b I like solving puzzles and I have a good memory.

c I enjoy detective stories.

Could you plan an excavation and lead a team?

a I'm a good organizer and communicator; people like working with me.

b I'm a great team player, but rather scatty and bad at planning ahead.

c I prefer to work quietly and peacefully, alone.

ANSWERS:

Mostly a: You're adventurous, observant, quick-thinking, well-organized—and you love history. Looks like you've got what it takes to lead a team of archaeological explorers.

Mostly b: If you wanted to, you could improve your skills and have adventures as an archaeologist.

Mostly c: At the moment, archaeological expeditions are not the best place for you. But perhaps, one day, you will learn to love treasures from past times.

GLOSSARY

acoustic using soundwaves; acoustic scanners bounce soundwaves off objects to create maps or 3D images on a screen

adapt change to suit the surrounding environment

ancestor someone from an earlier generation of a family

anthropology the study of cultures and lifestyles, both ancient and modern

antiquities ancient objects

archaeologist someone who studies the physical remains of the past

archaeology the study of objects, buildings, and landscapes left behind by past peoples

badlands dry countryside, where rocks have been worn into strange shapes by the wind and weather

CT-scan computerized tomography scan—a way of using X-rays to create images that show the inside of a solid object

DNA molecule found in the cells of all living things, that carries biological instructions (sometimes called the "genetic code") which tell cells how to live, function, and reproduce

excavation digging up

fossil remains of an animal or plant that lived long ago, which has been preserved in stone

founder person who starts or creates something

hieroglyphs type of picture writing used by the ancient Egyptians

hominid early human ancestor (all humans are members of the hominid family)

llama animal related to the camel, native to South America

oceanographic concerned with ocean mapping, study, and exploration

paleontologist someone who studies prehistoric life

papyrus early type of paper, made from reed-plants

prehistoric from a time long ago, before records began

ROV remotely operated vehicle—an unmanned underwater boat, fitted with lights, cameras, and sensors, and controlled by a distant operator

submersible mini-submarine, designed to carry explorers to very deep waters

terracotta baked clay

underdeveloped without good housing, roads, transport, power supplies, water, schools, hospitals, or jobs.

FIND OUT MORE

Books

Barber, Nicola. *Tomb Explorers* (Treasure Hunters). Chicago: Capstone, 2013.

Noon, Steve. *Story of the Titanic*. New York: Dorling Kindersley, 2012.

Hawass, Zahi. *Tutankhamun: The Mystery of the Boy King*. Washington, D.C.: National Geographic Books, 2007.

O'Connor, Jane. *Hidden Army: Clay Soldiers of Ancient China* (All Aboard Reading). New York: Penguin Books, 2011.

Sereno, Paul and Lunis, Natalie. *Supercroc*. New York: Bearport Publishing, 2007.

Websites

www.mummytombs.com/mummylocator/group/inca.htm
Site about Incan mummies in general.

www.nationalgeographic.com/explorers/bios/constanza-ceruti/
Information about Constanza Ceruti.

www.nationalgeographic.com/explorers/bios/paul-sereno/
Information about Paul Sereno.

**www.nationalgeographic.com/explorers/bios/
robert-ballard/**
Information about Robert Ballard.

**www.nationalgeographic.com/explorers/bios/
zahi-hawass**
Information about Zahi Hawass.

**www.ted.com/talks/lang/eng/robert_ballard_on_
exploring_the_oceans.html**
Robert Ballard talks about ocean exploring.

**www.world-archaeology.com/features/tombs-of-the-
lords-of-sipan**
Exciting descriptions of the discovery of the tomb of the
Lord of Sipán.

DVD

Discovery Channel – *Titanic* Gift Pack (Go Entertain 2009)

INDEX

Alva, Walter 18–23, 42
Andes 36–41
Andrews, Roy
   Chapman 7, 42
Anning, Mary 13
Arnold, Dieter 25

Ballard, Robert 8–11,
   42
Bingham, Hiram 6, 42

Caracol 22, 42
Carter, Howard 5, 42
Ceruti, Constanza
   36–41, 42
China 30–5

dinosaurs 7, 12–17, 42

Egypt 5, 19, 24–9, 42
El Niño 41

Fawcett, Percy 6, 42
fossil finders 7, 12–17,
   42

Gobero 16–17
Great Pyramid, Giza
   26–9, 42
Great Wall of China 31

Hawass, Zahi 24–9, 42
Huaca Rajada 20–2
human remains 16–17,
   42

ice mummies 38–40
Incan people 6, 36–41

Jason Project 11
Jones, Indiana 7

Khufu 26

Leakey, Mary 16, 42
Lerner, Mark 27
Lintong county, China
   30–5
Llullaillaco, Mount
   36–41, 42

Machu Picchu 6, 42
Mayan people 22, 42
Moche people 18–23
Mongolia 7
mountaineer
   archaeologists 36–41
mummies 29, 38–40

Nemo, Captain 8

ocean explorers 8–11
Ötzi 38–9
Oviraptor 7

palaeontologists 12–17
Peru 18–23
Project Exploration 12
pyramids 24–9, 42

Qin Shi Huang 31–5

Reinhard, Johan 37–41,
   42
robot exploration 26–7
Rosetta Stone 25
ROVs (remotely
   operated vehicles)
   10–11

Sahara Desert 14–17,
   42
Sereno, Paul 12–17, 42
Sima Qian 32
Sipán, Lord of 18–23,
   42
South America 18–23,
   36–41, 42
submersibles 9–11
Supercroc 15, 42

Tanzania 16, 42
terracotta warriors
   30–5, 42
Titanic, RMS 8–11, 42
tomb defenders 18–23
Tutankhamun 5, 28, 42

Valley of the Kings 24,
   28
Verne, Jules 8

Wu Yongqi 35

Xi'an 30–5, 42